Cool

Midwestern Cooking

Easy and Fun Regional Recipes

Alex Kuskowski

visit us at www.abdopublishing.com

Published by ABDO Publishing Company, a division of ABDO, P.O. Box 398166, Minneapolis, Minnesota 55439. Copyright © 2014 by Abdo Consulting Group, Inc. International copyrights reserved in all countries. No part of this book may be reproduced in any form without written permission from the publisher. Super SandCastle™ is a trademark and logo of ABDO Publishing Company.

Printed in the United States of America, North Mankato, Minnesota
062013
092013

PRINTED ON RECYCLED PAPER

Editor: Liz Salzmann
Content Developer: Nancy Tuminelly
Cover and Interior Design and Production: Colleen Dolphin, Mighty Media, Inc.
Food Production: Desirée Bussiere
Photo Credits: Colleen Dolphin, Shutterstock

The following manufacturers/names appearing in this book are trademarks: Arm & Hammer®, Buitoni®, Old London®, Proctor Silex®, Pyrex®, Roundy's®, Swanson®, Wyler's®

Library of Congress Cataloging-in-Publication Data

Kuskowski, Alex.
  Cool Midwestern cooking : easy and fun regional recipes / Alex Kuskowski.
       p. cm. -- (Cool USA cooking)
  Audience: 008-012.
  Includes bibliographical references and index.
   ISBN 978-1-61783-830-9
  1. Cooking, American--Midwestern style--Juvenile literature. I. Title.
   TX715.2.M53K87 2014
   641.5977--dc23
                                    2013001906

Safety First!

Some recipes call for activities or ingredients that require caution. If you see these symbols ask an adult for help!

HOT STUFF!
This recipe requires the use of a stove or oven. Always use pot holders when handling hot objects.

SUPER SHARP!
This recipe includes the use of a sharp **utensil** such as a knife or grater.

NUT ALERT!
Some people can get very sick if they eat nuts. If you are cooking with nuts, let people know!

Cuisine Cooking

Each regional recipe can have a lot of **versions**. Many are **unique** to the cook. The recipes in this book are meant to give you just a taste of regional cooking. If you want to learn more about one kind of cooking, go to your local library or search online. There are many great recipes to try!

Contents

Discover Midwestern Eats!

Take some time to explore the heart of American cooking, the Midwest! It's all about flour, dairy, and meat. The Midwest produces a lot of the foods eaten all over the United States.

Some of the best farming in the world is in the Midwest. The rich soil helps farmers raise cattle and grow wheat. Midwestern cooks know how to use these ingredients. Their recipes include some of the most famous American foods, such as hot dogs and macaroni and cheese.

There is a lot to learn about foods from the Midwest. Use the recipes in this book to have your own feast. Try them all, or make up your own. Grab a chef's hat, it's time for a cooking adventure!

Learn About the Midwest

Regional cooking has a lot to do with where the ingredients and recipes are from. Every region has its own **culture**. What do you know about Midwestern culture and food?

Minnesota

Wild rice is a grain that grows along lakes and rivers. That's good for Minnesota. There are more than 15,000 lakes there. Wild rice is a regional favorite.

Missouri

A lot of foods in Missouri are local specialties. Two of the most famous are butter cake and toasted ravioli.

Iowa

Iowa is famous for corn. It produces more corn than any other state.

North Dakota

Farms cover about 90 percent of North Dakota. Sunflowers are one of the main crops.

South Dakota

The state **dessert** is a **kuchen**. It's a tasty coffee cake.

Oklahoma

Oklahoma's state animal is the American buffalo or bison. Buffalo meat can be a substitute for beef. It has less fat and more protein.

Wisconsin

People from Wisconsin are nicknamed "Cheese heads." No wonder! Wisconsin makes about one-fourth of the nation's cheese.

Kansas

Wheat is in bread, **pasta**, crackers, and cookies. A lot of that wheat comes from Kansas.

Nebraska

Kool-aid was invented in 1927 in Hastings, Nebraska.

Michigan

Michigan is known for its blueberries. They grow more than any other state!

Indiana

The pork **tenderloin** sandwich is an Indiana classic. The tenderloin is breaded and fried and served on bread or a bun. It is often eaten with French fries.

Illinois

Cracker Jack and Vienna Beef hot dogs were first served in Illinois. They were introduced at the 1893 Chicago World's Fair.

Ohio

Ohio's favorite treat is peanut butter dipped in chocolate. It's nicknamed the "Buckeye" after the nuts from the state tree.

The Basics

Ask Permission

Before you cook, ask **permission** to use the
kitchen, cooking tools, and ingredients. If you'd
like to do something yourself, say so. Just
remember to be safe. If you would like help, ask
for it. Always ask for help using a stove or oven.

Be Prepared

- Be organized. Knowing where everything is makes
cooking easier and safer.

- Read the directions all the way through before you
start. Remember to follow the directions in order.

- The most important ingredient in great cooking
is preparation! Set out all your ingredients before
starting.

Be Neat and Clean

- Start with clean hands, clean tools, and a clean
work surface.

- Tie back long hair so it stays out of the food.

- Wear comfortable clothing. Roll up long sleeves.

Be Smart, Be Safe

- Never work in the kitchen if you are home alone.

- Always have an adult close by for hot jobs, such as using the oven or the stove.

- Have an adult around when using a sharp tool, such as a knife or grater. Always be careful when using them!

- Remember to turn pot handles toward the back of the stove. That way you won't accidentally knock them over.

Cool Cooking Terms

Peel
Peel means to remove the skin, often with a peeler.

Chop
Chop means to cut into small pieces.

Boil
Boil means to heat liquid until it begins to bubble.

Dice / Cube
Dice and *cube* mean to cut something into small squares.

Slice
Slice means to cut food into pieces of the same thickness.

Grate
Grate means to shred something into small pieces using a grater.

Core
Core means to cut the middle out of something.

Drain
Drain means to remove liquid using a strainer or colander.

The Tool Box

Here are some of the tools that you'll need for the recipes in this book.

9 × 13-inch baking dish	baking sheet	frying pan
electric mixer	measuring cups & spoons	mixing bowls
mixing spoon	pot holders	saucepans
slotted spoon	tongs	whisk

The Ingredients

Here are some of the ingredients that you'll need for the recipes in this book.

apples

baking soda

beef bouillon cubes

blueberries

bread crumbs

brown sugar

butter

carrots

celery

cheddar cheese

cheese ravioli

chicken broth

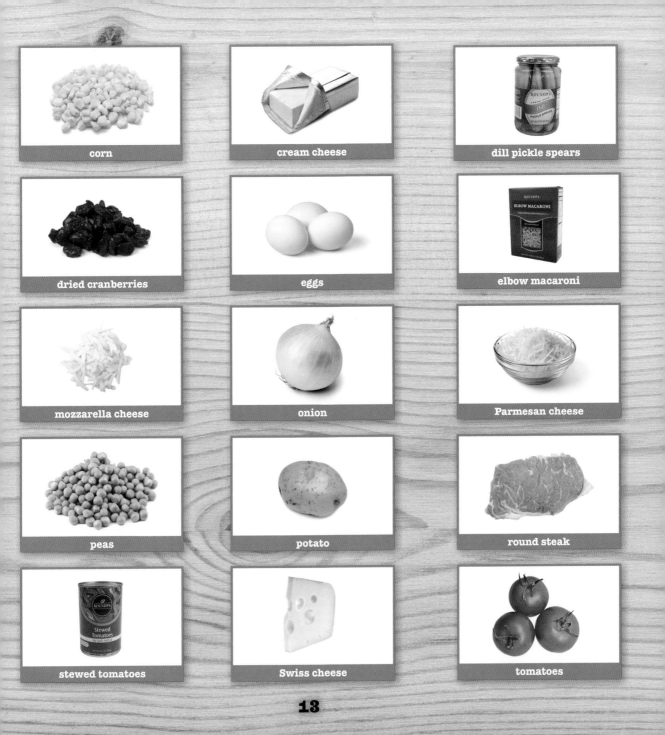

corn

cream cheese

dill pickle spears

dried cranberries

eggs

elbow macaroni

mozzarella cheese

onion

Parmesan cheese

peas

potato

round steak

stewed tomatoes

Swiss cheese

tomatoes

Moist & Delicious Butter Cake

Have a slice of this crumbly cake!

Makes 24 servings

Ingredients

non-stick cooking spray
1 cup butter
¼ cup milk
4 eggs
18.25-ounce package
  yellow cake mix
8 ounces cream cheese
2 cups powdered sugar
½ cup blueberries

Tools

9 × 13-inch baking dish
measuring cups
mixing bowls
electric mixer
mixing spoon
pot holders

1. Preheat the oven to 350 degrees. Coat the baking dish with non-stick cooking spray.

2. Put the butter, milk, and 2 eggs in a large mixing bowl. Beat together with the mixer. Stir in the cake mix. Pour the batter evenly into the baking dish.

3. Put the cream cheese and 2 eggs in a medium mixing bowl. Beat together with the mixer. Slowly add the powdered sugar. Mix well.

4. Pour the cream cheese mixture evenly over the cake batter. Bake for 35 minutes, or until the top starts to brown. Take it out and let it cool. Serve it with powdered sugar and blueberries.

hot!

Tip: Stick a toothpick in the cake. If it comes out clean, the cake is done!

Hearty Heartland Stew

Savory, smooth, and delicious!

Makes 8 servings

Ingredients

½ cup plus 2 tablespoons butter
½ cup flour
½ cup diced carrots
1 cup chopped onion
½ cup diced celery
1 potato, chopped
½ cup peas
½ cup corn
8-ounce can stewed tomatoes
6 beef bouillon cubes
¼ pound round steak, chopped
¼ teaspoon black pepper
2 tablespoons steak sauce

Tools

large saucepan
measuring cups
mixing spoon
frying pan
measuring spoons
sharp knife
cutting board

*hot!
*sharp!

1 Put ½ cup butter in a large saucepan. Heat over medium-high heat. Once the butter is melted, add the flour. Stir constantly until the mixture turns brown. It takes about 5 minutes.

2 Slowly add 2 cups water. Stir until the mixture is smooth.

3 Add the carrots, onion, celery, potato, peas, corn, tomatoes, bouillon, and 2 cups water.

4 Heat until the mixture boils. Then turn the heat to low.

5 Put 2 tablespoons butter in a frying pan. Heat over high heat until it is melted. Add the steak. Cook until the steak pieces are completely brown.

6 Put the cooked steak in the saucepan. Cover and cook over low heat for 90 minutes. Add pepper and steak sauce.

Windy City Hot Dog

Grab one for your next ball game!

Makes 1 serving

Ingredients

1 seven-grain hot dog bun
1 hot dog
1 tablespoon yellow mustard
1 tablespoon pickle relish
1 tablespoon diced onion
1 tomato, sliced
1 dill pickle spear
½ teaspoon celery salt

Tools

baking sheet
small saucepan
tongs
measuring cups
measuring spoons
sharp knife
cutting board
pot holders

*hot!
*sharp!

1 Preheat the oven to 300 degrees.

2 Place the hot dog bun on a baking sheet. Put it in the oven for 2 minutes. Remove it and set it aside.

3 Fill the saucepan with water. Bring to a boil over high heat. Turn the heat to medium. Add the hot dog. Cook for 5 minutes.

4 Use tongs to move the hot dog from the pan to the hot dog bun. Add yellow mustard in a zigzag.

5 Layer on the pickle relish, onion, tomato, and pickle spear. Sprinkle on the celery salt. One bite and you'll feel like you're at Wrigley field!

Even Cooler!

Try it on a poppy seed bun and add sport peppers for an **authentic** ballpark taste!

Wonderful Wild Rice Pilaf

A new taste and texture you'll love!

Makes 8 servings

Ingredients

1 cup walnuts
1 tablespoon olive oil
½ cup chopped onion
½ cup chopped carrots
½ cup peas
½ cup dried cranberries
½ teaspoon salt
4 cups chicken broth
1 cup white rice
¾ cup wild rice

Tools

measuring cups
baking sheet
sharp knife
cutting board
measuring spoons
small frying pan
mixing spoon
large saucepan with cover
pot holders

1 Preheat the oven to 350 degrees.

2 Put the walnuts on the baking sheet in a single layer. Bake for 8 minutes. Take them out. After they cool, chop them.

3 Put the olive oil in a small frying pan. Heat over medium heat for 1 minute. Add the onion, carrots, peas, cranberries, and salt. Stir and cook 5 minutes. Remove from heat and let it cool.

4 Put the broth, white rice, and wild rice in a large saucepan. Bring to a boil over high heat.

5 Turn the heat to low. Cover the pan. Cook for 40 minutes.

6 Stir the chopped walnuts and cooked vegetables into the rice mixture.

*hot!
*sharp!
*nuts!

Fried Ravioli Pasta

A mouthwatering specialty!

Makes 6 servings

Ingredients

1 egg

2 tablespoons milk

1 cup bread crumbs

½ tablespoon oregano

½ tablespoon chopped parsley

½ teaspoon salt

12.5-ounce package
cheese ravioli

3 cups vegetable oil

1 tablespoon grated Parmesan
cheese

16 ounces spaghetti sauce

Tools

2 small mixing bowls

measuring spoons

whisk

measuring cups

medium saucepan

large frying pan

tongs

slotted spoon

paper towels

serving bowl

hot!

1 Whisk the egg and milk together in a small mixing bowl. Put the bread crumbs, oregano, parsley, and salt in a separate mixing bowl. Stir.

2 Dip each ravioli in the egg mixture. Then coat it with the bread crumb mixture.

3 Put the oil in a frying pan. Heat over medium heat. Use tongs to carefully put the ravioli in the oil. Fry 1 minute. Use a slotted spoon to flip the ravioli. Fry the other side for 1 minute.

4 Place the ravioli on paper towels. Pat them to remove extra oil. Top them with Parmesan cheese.

5 Put the spaghetti sauce in a saucepan. Heat it until bubbles begin to appear. Turn off the heat. Pour the sauce into a serving bowl. Serve as a dip for the ravioli!

Delectable Mac & Cheese

Have a bite of an American classic!

Makes 8 servings

Ingredients

non-stick cooking spray
16-ounce package elbow macaroni
1½ cups grated mozzarella cheese
1 cup grated cheddar cheese
½ cup grated Parmesan cheese
½ cup grated Swiss cheese
½ cup ricotta cheese
½ cup sour cream
¾ cup heavy cream
1 tablespoon chopped parsley
½ teaspoon garlic salt

Tools

9 × 13-inch baking dish
large saucepan
colander
measuring cups & spoons
2 mixing bowls
mixing spoon
small bowl
cutting board
sharp knife
pot holders

*hot!
*sharp!

1   Preheat the oven to 400 degrees. Coat the baking dish with non-stick cooking spray.

2   Fill a large saucepan with water. Bring it to a boil. Add the macaroni. Cook for 6 minutes. Drain the macaroni.

3   Put the mozzarella, cheddar, Parmesan, and Swiss cheeses in a mixing bowl. Stir. Set ½ cup of the cheese mixture aside in a small bowl.

4   Put the ricotta cheese, sour cream, heavy cream, parsley, and garlic salt in a separate mixing bowl. Stir well. Add the ricotta mixture to the cheese mixture.

5   Stir in the macaroni. Spread the mixture evenly in the baking dish. Sprinkle the cheese mixture in the small bowl on top.

6   Bake for 10 minutes or until the cheese is melted. Turn the oven to broil. Broil for 5 minutes to brown the top.

Great Plains Cookies

Cinnamon cookies with a tasty crunch!

Makes 30 cookies

Ingredients

non-stick cooking spray
½ cup butter
½ cup vegetable oil
½ cup powdered sugar
¾ cup sugar
1 egg
1 teaspoon vanilla extract
2¼ cups flour
½ teaspoon salt
½ teaspoon baking soda
½ teaspoon cream of tartar
2 teaspoons cinnamon

Tools

baking sheet
measuring cups
mixing bowls
electric mixer
measuring spoons
mixing spoon
pot holders

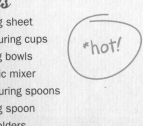

hot!

1. Preheat the oven to 375 degrees. Coat a baking sheet with non-stick cooking spray.

2. Put the butter, oil, powdered sugar, and ½ cup sugar in a large bowl. Beat until smooth. Beat in the egg and vanilla.

3. Put the flour, salt, baking soda, and cream of tartar in a medium bowl. Stir. Gradually add the flour mixture to the butter mixture. Beat thoroughly.

4. Mix the cinnamon and ¼ cup sugar in a small bowl.

5. Roll about 2 tablespoons of dough into a ball. Then roll the ball in the cinnamon sugar.

6. Place the balls on the baking sheet 2 inches (5 cm) apart. When the sheet is full, bake for 8 to 10 minutes. The cookies should be golden brown.

7. Repeat steps 5 and 6 until the dough runs out.

Apple Crisp Delight

Flavor you can savor!

Makes 8 servings

Ingredients

non-stick cooking spray

6 apples, cored, peeled, and sliced into wedges

½ teaspoon cinnamon

3 tablespoons white sugar

1 cup uncooked oatmeal

⅛ teaspoon salt

½ cup butter

¾ cup brown sugar

½ cup flour

Tools

8-inch square baking dish

measuring spoons

mixing spoon

measuring cups

large mixing bowl

fork

cutting board

sharp knife

pot holders

*hot!
*sharp!

1 Preheat the oven to 350 degrees. Coat the baking dish with non-stick cooking spray.

2 Put the apples in the baking dish. Sprinkle the cinnamon and sugar over the top. Stir to coat the apples evenly.

3 Put the remaining ingredients in a large bowl. Mix with a fork. Press the back of the fork into the mixture to create small clumps.

4 Pour the oatmeal mixture evenly over the apples. Bake for 35 minutes.

Even Cooler!

Serve warm with vanilla ice cream!

Conclusion

Now you know how to make some wonderful Midwestern dishes! Did you learn anything about Midwestern **cuisine**? Did you try any new foods? Everywhere you go there are new foods to experience.

From coast to coast the United States is a land of **delicious** dishes! East Coast, Pacific Coast, Gulf Coast, Midwest, South, and West are the main regions of US cuisine. Try them all to get a taste of the United States. See if one is your favorite!

Glossary

authentic – real or true.

cuisine – a style of preparing and presenting food.

culture – the behavior, beliefs, art, and other products of a particular group of people.

delicious – very pleasing to taste or smell.

dessert – a sweet food, such as fruit, ice cream, or pastry, served after a meal.

kuchen – one of several types of German desserts and pastries. Kuchen is the German word for cake.

pasta – a food made of dough that is formed into different shapes. It is usually boiled and served with a sauce.

permission – when a person in charge says it's okay to do something.

tenderloin – a cut of beef or pork from along the backbone.

unique – different, unusual, or special.

utensil – a tool used to prepare or eat food.

version – a different form or type from the original.

Web Sites

To learn more about regional US cooking, visit ABDO Publishing Company online at www.abdopublishing.com. Web sites about easy and fun regional recipes are featured on our Book Links page. These links are routinely monitored and updated to provide the most current information available.

Index